"MY"
OFFICIAL
CORNMEAL
"HOECAKES"

Bread and Accompaniments

Cookbook Of Seminole County

Before the

Statehood of Oklahoma

"MY"
OFFICIAL
CORNMEAL
"HOECAKES"

Bread and Accompaniments
Cookbook Of Seminole County
Before the
Statehood of Oklahoma

With Seminole Freedmen History Interests

SHARON HUNT

ISBN: Softcover   978-1-9845-2806-3
         eBook   978-1-9845-2805-6

Print information available on the last page.

Rev. date: 05/11/2018

To order additional copies of this book, contact:
Xlibris
1-888-795-4274
www.Xlibris.com
Orders@Xlibris.com
747919

CONTENTS

PART VI

PART VII

PART VIII

PART IX

PART X

PART XI

PART XII

PART XX

PART XXI

PART XXII

PART XXIII

PART XXIV

PART XXV

PART XXVI

PART XXVII

PART XXVIII

PART XXIX

PART XXX

PART XXXI

PART XXXII

PART XXXIII

PART XXXIV

DEDICATIONS

First and far most, the author dedicates this work
to JESUS CHRIST, OUR SAVIOUR.

This cookbook is dedicated to her grandmother
IDA B. FRAZIER, her father's mother.

Also, dedicated to her mother and father, Dewey
and Repol B. Hunt and her brothers.

The cookbook is dedicated to the SEMINOLE FREEDMEN.

ACKNOWLEDGEMENTS

The author wishes to thank the Seminole Freedmen who gave her oral histories about their ancestors and their contribution to Seminole county.

The author spent many days and nights with her mother and father traveling down the roads of the historic Seminole County. For years, the author traveled with her father around the area and her father pointed out all of the early settlers' contributions, their cemeteries and churches. Many times, she has visited "The River" and "Turkey Creek" and all the people.

Hopefully, this cookbook will serve as a resource to the young descendants and others to appreciate the wisdom of the Seminole Freedmen.

PREFACE

The Seminole Freedmen have more of an impact on America's history than what is known. However, in this cookbook the early food history, food selections and food preparation methods of the early settler of Seminole County are highlighted by showing the possible recipes for "hoecakes" and the cooking of these breads on a hoe either in the fireplace or camp fire.

The Seminole Freedmen were excellent cooks, interpreters for the Seminole Native Americans, Scouts for the United States Army and many more things.

However, what was of utmost importance was their beliefs in Jesus Christ and the setting up of churches.

DISCLAIMER

The menus and recipes are developed by the author. Oral histories are handed down from the generations of the people interviewed. The thoughts in the cookbook were given to the author and are opinions only.

According to some descendants, because the Seminole Freedmen were treated unfairly, not enough appreciation was given to them by the people they helped most. Therefore, the Seminole Freedmen were almost left out of the history books and dropped by the U.S. Government. It has been said that The Black Seminole Freedmen had been mistreated by the United States Government and the Seminole Native Americans. The Seminole Freedmen helped to win wars for both groups and served as interpreters for all of the Five Civilized Tribes.

INTRODUCTION

In this cookbook, the author will illustrate how the Seminole Freedmen prepared their popular bread -cornmeal hoecake and other menu items using a field hoe as a cooking tool while cooking in campfires and fireplaces. The Seminole Freedmen used this method of cooking as they were removed from Florida and traveled over the "Trail of Tears". In this cookbook, all menus will be written with the early settlers in mind. Also, the field hoe was used to chop and to clear land.

Each part of the cookbook has been outlined in the first section: Seminole Freedmen's early menus and recipes. The menus represent a possible first meal in their new home.

The second section will have information on the Seminole Freedmen staking their claims in Seminole County, Oklahoma-approximate year of settlement, types of people, names of settlers, name of settlement, whether slave to Seminole Native Americans or never a slave and some questions about their past in Florida, the First Seminole War, Second Seminole War and Third Seminole War. Selected scripture(s) will follow each chapter on the Seminole Freedmen

OKLAHOMA

1. STATEHOOD: November 16, 1907
2. CONSTITUTION: Oklahoma Constitution, 46th
3. Capital City: Oklahoma City
4. NICKNAME: Sooner State
5. Population (013): 2,850, 568 Rank: 28
6. BIRD: Scissor-Tailed Flycatcher
7. Flower: Mistletoe
8. Origin of State Name: Based of Choctaw Indian word for "Red Man".
9. Song: "Oklahoma" Words by: Oscar Hammerstein and music by: Richard Rodgers

10. TREE: Eastern Red Bud
11. Border States: Arkansas, Colorado, Kansas, Missouri, New Mexico, Texas
12. Lowest Point Little River at Arkansas border- 287 feet, 33rd lowest
13. AFRICAN-AMERICAN 2010 CENSUS IN OKLAHOMA: 277,644
14. HISTORICAL FACTS: INDIAN TERRITORY, OKLAHOMA TERRITORY
15. SEMINOLE COUNTY AND SEMINOLE FREEDMEN AND SEMINOLE NATIVE AMERICANS
16. Wewoka is the oldest Black City in Oklahoma and was found by a Black Man John Horse.

PART I

CORNMEAL "HOECAKES" BREAD AND ACCOMPANIMENT

SECTION I

MENU

Sorghum Molasses/Syrup Filler
Ash Hoecakes

RECIPES

Sorghum Molasses/Syrup Filler

Amounts	Ingredients
1 cup	molasses/syrup

Directions

1. Split hoecakes in half.
2. Place 1 tablespoon of syrup on each cooked hoe cake of bread half.
3. Fold hoecake to make a sandwich.
4. Eat the sandwich while hot.

   (Note: Sorghum cane was used to extract the juice to make the molasses. The cane is grown up to ripened and stripped then sent through a process to squeeze the juice.

The cane juice is cooked in syrup mill over a controlled heat for about 8 hours. The foam is skimmed until the molasses are complete. The molasses is used as a syrup for bread or a seasoning in cooking other foods.)

Ash Hoecakes

Amounts	Ingredients
3 cups	stoneground yellow cornmeal
1 tablespoon	salt
1 ½ cups	water
8	cabbage leaves

Directions

1. Make a campfire and let wood burn down to coals. Take a hoe and rake coals up in a small bed. Then make hoecakes to be cooked in the ashes.
2. In a large pan, stir all the ingredients.
3. Make 8 corn patties with hands.
4. Wrap each corn patty in a cabbage leaf or collard leaf.
5. Place filled leaf on the hoe blade and cook for 5 to 10 minutes on one side. Turn to cook on second side and cook 3 to 4 minutes.
6. Remove from heat with hoe.
7. Place on plate.
8. Repeat the process until all the cakes are done.
9. Remove bread from leaves. Discard leaves. Place molasses in the center of each cake.
10. Make a sandwich and eat hot.

SECTION II

SEMINOLE FREEDMEN

1829 (Approximate Settlement Year in Seminole County)
BRUNERS(FROM FLORIDA SETTLEMENT FORT MOSE)
SALT CREEK

1. Cities, Communities, Settlement: Little River - Salt Creek
2. Names of People: Bruners -William(Paden) and Affie to Indian Territory around 1829 over the Trail of Tears. Alfie was related to Abram Lincoln an interpreter for the Seminole Indians. The family probably left after the First Seminole War in 1818 in Florida

   Against the free black community. In 1821 United States acquired Florida from Spain.

   These were Ceasar Bruner parents.

3. Type of People: The people were probably from Fort Mose-Spanish Free Blacks, maroons, Seminole Indian and slave mixed and Seminole Freedmen.

   Note: A city called Mose was the first legally sanctioned free black town in America. The inhabitants were black fugitives from Georgia, Virginia and the Carolinas. As a result of the American Revolution(1775-1782), the black fugitives and American Indians grew closer.

   The area was known as Fort Mose and the freedom was granted by Spain. When Florida became a state, the blacks left in the early 1820s.

4. Distance of place from county seat of Wewoka: almost12 miles
5. Short History:

13

The Bruner couple came to Indian Territory as a result of

President Andrew Jackson removing Seminole Indians

From Florida, the white slave owners trying to catch run-a-way or escaped slaves from the states of Georgia, South Carolina and North Carolina and the United States government annexed the State of Florida and the freed slaves left for Oklahoma Territory. The African-Americans were Gullah-speaking people.

They probably were slaves descendants stolen from the areas of the Congo, and West Africa.

The War of 1812, General Andrew Jackson attacked the Fort Mose and ran the blacks off. Also in the First Seminole War (1804 -1814) the Blacks and Indians had to flee.

6. The couple probably traveled to Seminole County from Hughes County with the Creeks.

   The couple probably got on a steam ship and traveled up to New Orleans then to the Arkansas River and then got off the boat and got on a wagon train and then rode horses up to Salt Creek.

   The Seminole Indians were trying to fight the whites from capturing the escaped or run-a- way slaves.

7. What foods did they have with them? They probably had limited food with them. They probably had ground meal and molasses syrup.
8. What other things did they have? They probably had a flint rock, a hoe without a handle and a food grinder.

9. Questions to be asked:

   1. How did the families know about the lower part of Seminole County.
   2. Did some of the Seminole Freedmen travel with the Spanish explorers to find the area?

10. Who were the first Seminole Freedmen to come to Indian Territory?

The area was known as The Indian Territory before 1889. After 1889 the area was called Oklahoma Territory. Oklahoma became a state in 1907.

BIBLICAL SCRIPTURE:

GENESIS 49:25

Even by the God of thy father, who shall help thee and by the Almighty, who shall bless thee with blessings of heaven above, blessings of the deep that lieth under, blessings of breasts, and of the womb.

PART II

CORNMEAL "HOECAKES" BREAD AND ACCOMPANIMENT

MENU

Fried Pork Fatback
Hot Water Cornmeal Hoecake Bread

RECIPES

Fried Fatback

Amounts	Ingredients
2 pounds	Pork fatback sliced

Directions

1. Fry meat in black pot until crispy.
2. Eat with hot hoecake.

Hot Water Hoecake Bread

Amounts	Ingredients
2 cups	white cornmeal
1 teaspoon	salt
1 cup	hot water

Directions

1. Ground meal and place in a pan.
2. Stir in remaining ingredients.
3. Make into 8 patties.
4. Place on the blade of the hoe. One at a time. Cook in fireplace.
5. Cool. Slice in half and place meat between halves. Make sandwich. Serve.

SECTION II

SEMINOLE FREEDMEN

1838(Approximate Year of Settling in Seminole County)
ABRAHAM SETTLEMENT
The Negro Abraham settled Hazel near Little River west of the Little River Settlement

1. Cities, Communities and/ or Settlement: Hazel, Near Bowlegs
2. Name of Seminole Freedmen: Abraham, Interpreter for the Seminole Indians and a great warrior. He was a slave to and interpreter to Chief Micanopy. He was a great warrior. Ceasar Bruner was the son-in-law to Abraham.
3. Types of People: Abraham was a slave to Seminole Indians and Emancipation Proclamation. He got his land from the Seminoles emancipation.
4. Name of Town: Hazel
5. Short History:

   Abraham was an interpreter for the Seminoles. He served the Chief in the Second and Third Seminole Wars. Abraham probably traveled in a wagon train up from Fort Gibson.

   He probably helped to hunt for game animals and cooked food over coals in the fire place.

   Abraham once visited Wewoka.

6. Abraham is buried in the first Bruner Town cemetery. He was a member of the Seminole Nation from the beginning in Florida. He helped the Seminole Indians to fight in the wars.
7. The Indians called him "Souanaffe Tustenukke" a ranking member. Even though, Abraham was a full blooded Negro, he was an interpreter, counsellor, war leader and diplomat.
8. Was Abraham an Indian Scout?
9. Where did they get their horses and mules from?

SCRIPTURE: PSALM 1:1-3

"Blessed is the man that walketh not in the counsel of the ungodly, nor standeth in the way of sinner, nor sitteth in the seat of the scornful. But his delight is in the law of the Lord, and in his law doth he meditate day and night. And he shall be like a tree planted by the rivers of water, that bringeth forth his fruit in his season; his leaf also shall not wither, and WHATSOEVER HE DOETH SHALL PROSPER."

PART III

CORNMEAL "HOECAKES" BREAD AND ACCOMPANIMENT

SECTION I

MENU

Smothered Squirrel and Gravy
Cornmeal Hoecake and Flour Bread

RECIPES

Smothered Squirrel and Gravy

Amounts	Ingredients
1	squirrel, skinned and cut -up
1 tablespoon	salt
½ cup	flour
½ cup	lard

Directions

1. Skin, cut-up and wash squirrel. Pat dry.
2. Season with salt. Roll in flour.
3. Heat lard in a pan.
4. Place squirrel in hot lard. Cook on both sides.
5. Remove fully cooked squirrel from pan.
6. Remove most of the fat.
7. Sprinkle 1 tablespoon of flour in skillet.
8. Slowly stir in water and make gravy. Add cooked squirrel pieces back to the gravy. Stir and cover and simmer for 20 minutes.

Cornmeal and Flour Hoecakes

Amounts	Ingredients
1 cup	stoneground yellow cornmeal
1 cup	flour
1 teaspoon	salt
½ cup	water

Directions

1. In a pan, stir all ingredients together.
2. Make into 8 patties 2 -inches wide.
3. Place each on a hoe and cook until done.
4. Serve with smothered squirrel.

SECTION II

SEMINOLE FREEDMEN

1854s (Approximate Year of Settling in Seminole County)
BRUNER TOWN I COMMUNITY
Bruner Town on Salt Creek-midway between Seminole and Konawa
Caesar Bruner Band, a Seminole freedman never a slave to Seminole
Indians. He was born in Florida.

1. Cities, Communities and Settlements: Bruner Town
2. Name of Seminole Freedmen: Bruner Band headed by Caesar
   Bruner
3. Type of People: Escaped to freedom living in Florida
4. Short History:

   Caesar Bruner mother was the daughter of Abram Lincoln.
   Abram Lincoln was an interpreter for the Seminole Indians.
   Abram was the uncle of the warrior Osceola, a famous warrior
   of the Seminole tribe.

   Caesar Bruner came to Indian Territory from Florida with his
   parents.

   Son-in-law to Abraham. Brothers Caesar, Pavo, and William
   founded a small freedman community called Bruner Town.

   Caesar Bruner Band was named after Caesar Bruner, a freedman,
   who was born in Florida, but came to Indian Territory with his
   parents.

5. Bruner Cemetery I (OLD BRUNERTOWN CEMETERY-
   SEMINOLE NATION FREEDMEN- BOWLEGS,
   OKLAHOMA.)

   1. Grace Bowlegs -1825-1885 -Full blooded Seminole,
      wife of John Bruner

Born in Florida. Grace had four children: Ellen, Ben, Tom and Annie.

2. John Bruner 1824-1889. John, husband of Grace and father to Ellen, Ben, Tom and Annie. He came with his parents William, (Paden) and Affie to Indian Territory around 1829 over the historic "Trail of Tears". He and his brothers Caesar, Perry, Pavo and Williams founded a small Freedman community called Burner Town.

3. Additional names in cemetery: Alexander, Barnette, Bowlegs, Brown and Burner.

6. Church: Salt Creek Baptist Church?
7. What foods did the Bruners plant in their gardens?
8. Bruner had two stores at Heliswa. What did he have in his stores?
9. Did he have a smoke house? How did he preserve his fruits and vegetables?
10. How did he learn methods to plant crops?

BIBLICAL SCRIPTURE: MATTHEW 6:33

"But seek ye first the kingdom of God, and his righteousness, and all these things shall be added unto you."

PART IV

CORNMEAL "HOECAKES" BREAD AND ACCOMPANIEMENT

MENU

Boiled Turnip Greens with Dumplings
Cornmeal Hoecakes with Onions

RECIPES

Boiled Turnip Greens with Dumplings

Amounts	Ingredients
½ pound	cured meat, cubed
2 quarts	water
1 bunch	turnip greens
1 cup	yellow corn meal
1 teaspoon	salt

Directions

1. Place meat in a large black pot in the fireplace and add water and cook over medium coals for 2 hours.
2. Wash and cut up greens.
3. Stir greens and stir into the pot.
4. In a bowl, stir together, cornmeal. Salt and water. Make 1" balls and save for a minute.
5. Place the balls on top of greens and cover.
6. Do not stir cook on low heat for one hour. Serve.

Cornmeal Hoecake with Onions

Amounts	Ingredients
2 cups	cornmeal
1 teaspoon	salt
½ cup	water
¼ cup	onions, minced

Directions

1. In a pan, stir together all of the ingredients.
2. Make 8 stiff cornmeal patties.
3. Cook on top of the hoe's blade in the hot coals. One at a time.
4. Serve hot with greens.

SECTION II

SEMINOLE FREEDMEN

1840s(Approximate Time of Settling in Seminole County)
ROBERT JOHNSON COMMUNITY
4 Miles north of Wewoka
Robert Johnson served as an Interpreter and agent to Seminole Indians.

1. Cities, Communities and Settlements: Settled by Robert Johnson father of Lawyer James Coody Johnson
2. Type of People: Freed slaves from the Seminole Indians.
3. Robert Johnson was an Indian Agent. His son, James Coody Johnson was a Seminole and Creek Indian Agent. James Coody was a lawyer in Wewoka.
4. Robert Johnson was born in 1824 and died in 1893.
5. Johnson was probably a slave to The Thomas Palmer Band whose chief was Chief John F. Brown, the Last Chief before statehood.
6. People who may have traveled with Robert Johnson: Browns, Obys, Perrys, Bruners
7. Dan Brown was a lighthorse man, who served as a policeman.
8. Church: Pilgrims Rest Baptist Church
9. Who was the Seminole Indian Tribe were the Johnsons slaves to?
10. Johnson Cemetery: Robert Johnson Dec. 1824-Dec. 13, 1893, interpreter for Seminole Indians, Dan Brown, light horseman, Noble Bowlegs, Charley Brown
11. Did Johnson come with s wagon train from Fort Gibson?
12. How did he know where to settle?

BIBLICAL SCRIPTURE: II CHRONCILES 20:20

"Believe in the Lord your God, so shall ye be established; believe his prophets, SO SHALL YE PROSPER."

PART V

CORNMEAL "HOECAKES" BREAD AND ACCOMPANIMENT

SECTION I

MENU

Boiled Pinto Beans
Cornbread Hoecakes

RECIPES

Boiled	Pinto Beans
Amounts	Ingredients
2 cups	pinto beans, washed and picked
1	ham hock, cured
1 teaspoon	salt
1 tablespoon	sugar
2 quarts	water
½ teaspoon	red pepper flakes

Directions

1. In a large black pot, place all ingredients.
2. Stir well. Cover with lid and boil for 3 hours.
3. Test for doneness.

Cornmeal Hoecakes

Amounts	Ingredients
2 cups	yellow cornmeal
¼ cup	flour
1 cup	buttermilk
1 teaspoon	baking soda
1 teaspoon	salt
1 tablespoon	sugar

Directions

1. In a pan, stir together all the ingredients.
2. Heat up a tablespoon of lard in a pan.
3. Pour cornmeal in skillet, cook on low coals until done.

SECTION II

SEMINOLE FREEDMEN

1849 (Approximate time of Settling in Seminole County.)
WEWOKA
Discovered by John Horse in 1849 John Horse was a fighter he brought more than 200 people to Wewoka area.

1. Cities, Towns and Communities: Wewoka incorporated in 1866.
2. Types of People: Ex-Slaves from Florida.
3. Established by African-Seminole leader, John Horse and 200 others.
4. John Horse was probably a maroon. What Seminole Indians were known in his area?
5. The town had notable African-Seminole among its resident at one time Negro Abraham, Caesar Bruner, Dorsar Barkus and Cudjoe.
6. John Horse was the nephew of Osceola's second wife. Wewoka
7. The meaning of the word 'Wewoka' is said to be "Barking Waters".
8. Wewoka was incorporated in 1866,
9. County seat of Seminole County.
10. John Horse brought 200 people with him. He had Wild Cat with him.
11. John Horse left Wewoka and led many people and settled in Mexico.
12. John Horse was a brilliant fighter and was an Indian Scout.
13. How and why did John Horse come to Wewoka?
14. Who were the people did he bring with him?
15. What Seminole Indians did he know?
16. What types of foods did he have with him? Did he build a settlement of houses?
17. How long did he stay in Wewoka?
18. Did John Horse fight in the Second Seminole War?
19. How many women did they have with them?

20. Early churches in Wewoka-St. Joseph Baptist and St. Mathews Church.
21. Did John Horse settle on the north side of Wewoka Creek or the south side?
22. Did Wild Cat(Coacoochee) help to settle Wewoka with John Horse?
23. How did they know where to come? Had Desoto come to Wewoka before?

BIBLICAL SCRIPTURE: II THESSALONIANS 3:6

"Now we command you, brethren, in the name of our Lord Jesus Christ, that ye withdraw Yourselves from every brother that walketh disorderly, and not after the tradition, which he received of us."

PART VI

CORNMEAL "HOECAKES" BREAD AND ACCOMPANIEMENTS

MENU

Cornmeal Hoecake Bread
Buttermilk or Clabbered Milk Cup

RECIPES

Cornmeal Hoecakes Bread

Amounts	Ingredients
2 cups	yellow cornmeal
1 teaspoon	salt
1 tablespoon	sugar
¾ cup	buttermilk

Directions

1. In a bowl, stir together yellow corn meal, salt and sugar.
2. Stir in buttermilk.
3. Make into 6 corn patties and cook on a hoe until done.

Buttermilk or Clabbered Milk Cup (for one)

Amounts	Ingredients
1 ½ cups	buttermilk, cold
1 ½ teaspoons	sugar

Directions

1. Place cold buttermilk/clabbered milk in a bowl.
2. Crumble one patty in bowl of milk.
3. Add sugar and enjoy.

SECTION II

SEMINOLE FREEDMEN

1866 (Approximate time of Settling)
TURKEY CREEK
Near Little
EMANCIPATED SLAVES FROM SOUTHERN STATES
SETTLED ON TURKEY CREEK

In 1866 a group of emancipated African-Americans settled along Turkey Creek on about 320 acres. The freed slaves were Thomas and M. Benton

1. Cities, Towns and Communities: Turkey Creek Community
2. Types of People: Ex-slaves of white people and Seminole Indians
3. Ex-Slaves probably were given some money as reparation.
4. Did these people come from Fort Gibson?
5. What types of foods did they have?

"Wherefore seeing we also are compassed about with so great a cloud of witnesses, let us lay aside every weight, and the sin which doth so easily beset us, and let us run with patience the race that is set, looking unto Jesus the author and finisher of our faith, who for the joy that was set before Him endured the cross despising the shame, and is set down at the right hand of the throne of God."

PART VII

CORNMEAL "HOECAKES" BREAD AND ACCOMPANIMENT

MENU

Fried Corn
Cornmeal Pan Hoecake

Recipes

Fried Corn

Amounts	Ingredients
6 ears	yellow corn
¼ cup	butter
1 teaspoon	salt
2 tablespoons	flour
2 teaspoons	sugar

Directions

1. Wash and cut the corn three times from each of the cobs.
2. Heat butter in the skillet. Add the cut corn, salt, flour and sugar. Stir well.
3. Cook the corn in the skillet and remaining ingredients. Cook for about 10 minutes add water to keep from drying out.
4. Serve with cornmeal hoecake.

Cornmeal Hoecakes

Amount	Ingredients
2 cups	cornbread
1 teaspoon	salt
¼ cup	flour
1 teaspoon	baking powder
1 ½ teaspoons	sugar
1 cup	milk

Directions

1. In a bowl, stir together all ingredients, except milk and butter.
2. Stir in milk and butter.
3. Heat lard in a skillet in the fireplace. Heat until the lard slightly smokes.
4. Pour cornmeal mixture in skillet. Cook for 10 minutes and turn. Complete cooking.

SECTION II

SEMINOLE FREEDMEN

1870 (Approximate time of Settling)
BRUNER TOWN II COMMUNITY
Turkey Creek
(Second town settled by Ceasar Bruner moved his family from first location.)

1. Cities, Towns, Communities: BRUNER TOWN II COMMUNITY
2. Ceasar Bruner moved his family to a second location to raise cattle and to escape the violence from the first location. Ceasar Bruner, had seven boys and one girl, was the head of the Bruner Band until his death.
3. Ceasar Bruner established the Bruner Band. Caesar Bruner was the first band chief elected after the Civil War in 1865 and remained chief until his death.

Political Rules:

1-voting-Candidates had to be nominated and voted on.

4. Winner-The candidate with the most votes won the office.

Band Chief

1. All chiefs must be male.
2. Should be sufficient age and character.
3. Should have honor and able to serve.
4. Should be able to speak Seminole language.

Lighthorse men

1. Cesar Bruner established light horsemen to keep the law. One of his sons,

49

Tecumseh- a light horseman and one of his sons shot and killed one of his brothers because the brother refused to be arrested by Tecumseh.

The company of Light Horsemen shall consist of one captain, one lieutenant, and eight privates in all ten men. Famous light horsemen were T. Bruner, Caesar Payne, Pomp Davis, Tom Payne, Thomas Bruner, Dennis Cyrus and Sam Cudjo

3. Ceasar Bruner established the Mount Zion Church and the Mount Zion Church Cemetery

5. Bruner II Cemetery at Little, Seminole County: names-Caesar Bruner, Grant Tecumsah "G.T." Bruner-1875-1924.(Caesar's son and a lighthorseman), Benjamin Franklin Bruner, Douglas Bruner, Elmer (Bob) Bruner, Edwards, Glass, and Sneeds.

BIBLICAL SCRIPTURE: I THESSALONIANS 5:22

"Abstain from ALL APPEARANCE of evil"

PART VIII

CORNMEAL "HOECAKES" BREAD AND ACCOMPANIMENT

MENU

Cornmeal Hoecake and Goat milk with Wild Black Berries

RECIPES

Cornmeal Hoecakes Bread

Amounts	Ingredients
2 cups	white corn meal
1 teaspoon	salt
1 teaspoon	baking soda
2 tablespoons	flour
1 tablespoon	sugar
1 cup	milk

Directions

1. In a pan, stir together cornmeal, salt, baking soda, sugar and flour.
2. Stir in milk.
3. Make into six patties and cook individual on a hoe.
4. Cook done.

Goat Milk with Wild Blackberries

Amounts	Ingredients
5 cups	goat milk
4 cups	wild blackberries
2 ½ tablespoons	sugar

Directions

1. Place hoecake patties in each of the small bowls.
2. Place 1 cup of milk in each on top of each pattie.
3. Measure out ½ cup wild blackberries on top of the goat milk.
4. Sprinkle 1 teaspoon sugar on top of berries.

SECTION II

SEMINOLE FREEDMEN

1850s (Approximate time of Settling in Seminole County.)
Sasakwa Town
Freed slaves from Seminole Indians
Home of Gov. John F. Brown for 34 years. Principal Chief of the
Seminole Nation, succeeding his father-in-law, Chief John Jumper, Col
1st Reg. Seminole.

1. Cities, Towns and Communities: Sasakwa
2. Type of People: Seminole freedmen who were freed by the
   Seminole Indians.
3. The United States Government freed slaves in 1865. The Treaty
   of 1866 was made with the Five Civilized Tribes and the Indians
   were told to give their former slaves citizenship and their rights.
   The ex-slaves became known as the Indian freedmen and their
   descendant were also freedmen.
4. Spring Hill Baptist Church?
5. What foods did they bring with them?
6. What group of Seminole Indians were they slave to?
7. Did they received land from the Seminole Indians?

BIBLICAL SCRIPTURE: COLOSSIANS 3:17

"And whatsoever ye do in word or deed do all in the name of the Lord
Jesus, giving thanks to God and the Father by him."

PART IX

CORNMEAL "HOECAKES" BREAD AND ACCOMPANIMENT

MENU

Smothered Wild Onions
Cornmeal Hoecake

RECIPES

Smothered Wild Onions

Amounts	Ingredients
4 bunches	wild onions, washed and cut up
1 quart	water
2 tablespoons	lard
1 dozen	eggs, beaten
1 ½ teaspoons	salt

Directions

1. Wash and cut up wild onions. Boil in water until tender.
2. Drain water from onions. Heat lard in a skillet. Place onions and eggs in the skillet.
3. Scramble for 10 minutes and season with the salt.

Cornmeal Hoecakes

Amounts	Ingredients
2 cups	corn meal
1 cup	flour
1 teaspoon	salt
1 teaspoon	baking soda
1 cup	milk
1	egg, beaten
2 tablespoons	lard, melted

Directions

1. In a pan, place cornmeal, flour, salt and baking soda. Stir well.
2. Add milk, egg and lard.
3. Stir in cornmeal mixture. Pour into pan and cook in the fireplace until done.
4. Cut bread into slices.
5. Serve with wild onions on top of bread.

SECTION II

SEMINOLE FREEDMEN

1870s(Approximate Time of Settling in Seminole County)
THOMAS TOWN COMMUNITY
Northwest of Sasakwa

1. Cities, Town and Communities: THOMAS TOWN COMMUNITY
2. Types of People: Freed slaves from Seminole Indians from Florida.
3. Thomas Town Cemetery established in 1876. Thomas Town Cemetery is on Tate Mountain.
4. Cemetery established by Abe Thomas:

   Names in cemetery: Abraham, Barkus, Cudjo, Payne, Bruner, Carolina, Davis, Sango, Dindy, Garfield, Huntley, Lottie, Lancaster, Olden, Pompey, Roberts, Warrior, Sears, Abe Thomas, Lancaster, Ceaser Payne, Mundy Dindy, Barkus, Celia Payne Bruner and Thomas N. Thomas

5. Short History: Thomas Town was settled because of escaped slaves escaping the Second Seminole War. The Seminole Freedmen lived among the Seminole Indians.
6. What foods did they bring with them from Florida? Were they involved in the Second Seminole War?
7. Church-Thomas Town Baptist Church?
8. Did they get their land from the Dawes Roll?

BIBLICAL SCRIPTURE: I CORINTHIANS 10, 21, 23, 31

"Ye cannot drink the cup of the Lord, and the cup of devils, ye cannot be partakers of the Lord's table, and of the table of devils...All things are lawful for me, but all things edify not...Whether therefore ye eat, or drink, or whatsoever ye do, do all to the glory of God."

PART X

CORNMEAL "HOECAKES" BREAD AND ACCOMPANIEMENT

SECTION I

MENU

Fried Rabbit
Cornmeal Hoecake Pones

RECIPES

Fried Rabbit

Amounts	Ingredients
1	rabbits, skinned, washed and cut up
2 teaspoons	salt
2 cups	flour
2 cups	lard

Directions

1. Skin, wash and cut up rabbit.
2. Salt and flour rabbit.
3. Heat up lard to hot. Fry rabbit pieces to crispy.

Cornmeal Hoecake Pones

Amounts	Ingredients
2 cups	yellow cornmeal
¼ cup	flour
1 teaspoon	salt
1 teaspoon	baking soda
½ cup	buttermilk
1 cup	lard for frying

Directions

1. In a pan, stir together, flour, salt and baking soda.
2. Stir in buttermilk.
3. Make into 3 inch pones.
4. Fry in hot lard until golden brown.

SECTION II

SEMINOLE FREEDMEN

1850s(Approximate Time of Settling in Seminole County)
BOWLEGS TOWN
SEMINOLE FREEDMEN -Slaves freed by Seminole Indians by emancipation of slaves. Slaves of Billy Bowlegs(Halpatter Micco). He had 50 slaves.

Family of Ben Bruno, a slave who was an interpreter for the Seminole Indians

1. Cities, Towns, Communities: Bowlegs name of Billy Bowlegs, a leader of the Seminoles in Florida.
2. Type of People: Former slaves freed by the Seminole Indians
3. Caesar Bowlegs was a Seminole Freedman who was important to the Seminole Indians and the Seminole Freedmen. Bowlegs and his parents were born slaves of Eliza Bowlegs.
4. He was a mail man from Fort Gibson, he was an assistant to white medical doctors. He helped the doctors to vaccinate against smallpox in the Seminole Nation. In his later years, he operated a draw bridge over the Wewoka Creek.

BIBLICAL SCRIPTURE: ROMANS 14:23

"Whatsoever is not of faith is sin."

67

PART XI

CORNMEAL "HOECAKES" AND ACCOMPANIENT

MENU

Rabbit Soup
Cornmeal Hoecake

RECIPES

Rabbit Soup

Amounts	Ingredients
1	rabbit, skinned, cut up, washed
2 quarts	water
3 cups	tomatoes, chopped
2	hot peppers, chopped
1 teaspoon	salt

Directions

1. Skin, wash and cut up rabbit. Place in water and boil.
2. Add tomatoes, hot peppers and salt.
3. Place top on the pot and boil for 2 hours.

SECTION II

SEMINOLE FREEDMAN

1890s(Approximate Time of Settling Seminole County)
TIDMORE(now Seminole)

1. Cities, Towns, Communities: Tidmore
2. Types of People: Ex-slaves freed by the Seminole Indians
3. Tidmore later own was renamed Seminole.

BIBLICAL SCRIPTURES: I CORINTHIANS 6:1, 19, 20

"All things are lawful unto me, but all things are not expedient: all things are

Lawful for me, but I will not be brought under the power of any......
What?

Know ye not that your body is the temple of the Holy Ghost which is in you, which Ye have of God, and ye are not your own? For ye are bought with a price: therefore glorify God In your body, and in your spirit which are God's."

PART XII

CORNMEAL "HOECAKES" BREAD
AND ACCOMPANIMENT

SECTION I

MENU

Fried Carp Fish
Cornmeal Hoecake

RECIPES

Fried Carp Fish

Amounts	Ingredients
6 small	fish
2 teaspoons	salt
4 cups	cornmeal
4 cups	lard

Directions

1. Clean fish and wash. Pat dry season with salt.
2. Roll in cornmeal.
3. Put lard in skillet heat until hot.
4. Fry until crispy.

Cornmeal Hoecakes

Amounts	Ingredients
2 cups	cornmeal
1 cup	flour
1 teaspoon	baking soda
1 teaspoon	salt
1 cup	milk

Directions

1. Place cornmeal, flour, baking soda, salt
2. In a bowl, stir in milk.

SECTION II

1870s(Approximate Time in Settling in Seminole County)
LIMA

1. Cities, Towns, Communities: Black Town-One of the few all black townships in Oklahoma still existing. Located 6 miles south of city of Seminole and located in Seminole County.
2. Lima had public schools.
3. People who settled the community: Islands, Hills, Hubbards, Hardemans, Louies, Keese, Blanton, Davis, Dunlap, Edwards, Freeman, Shelton, Griffis, Gross, Overstreet,
4. History: Lima is located in Seminole County south of U.S. Highway 270 on County Road. Lima was incorporated in 1904. However, the community was there before the incorporation.

BIBLICAL SCRIPTURES: I CORINTHIANS 8:9 9, 11-13

"But take heed lest by any means this liberty of yours become a stumbling block to them that are weak…And through thy knowledge shall they weak brother perish, for whom Christ died? But when ye sin so against the brethren, and wound their weak conscience, ye sin against Christ. Wherefore, if meat make my brother to offend, I will eat no flesh while the world standeth, lest I make my brother to offend."

PART XIII

CORNMEAL "HOECAKES" BREAD AND ACCOMPANIMENT

MENU

Fried Bass Fish
Cornmeal Hoecakes

RECIPES

Fried Bass Fish

Amounts	Ingredients
3 pounds	bass fish, cleaned and washed
2 tablespoons	salt
2 cups	yellow cornmeal
2 cups	lard

Directions

1. Scale, Clean and wash fish.
2. Season with salt
3. Roll in flour.
4. Heat lard in a skillet.
5. Fry each fish until golden brown.

Cornmeal Hoecakes

Amounts	Ingredients
2 cups	cornmeal
2 tablespoons	salt
¼ cup	onion, minced
1 cup	water

Directions

1. Mix together, cornmeal and salt in a pan. Stir in water.
2. Make into a 8 patties.
3. Cook on top of a hoe in coals.

SECTION II

SEMINOLE FREEDMEN

1890s(Approximate Time of Settling in Seminole County.)
ARBEKA COMMUNITY
Located in northeastern corner of Seminole County

1. Cities, Towns, Community: ARBEKA COMMUNITY
2. Type of People: Creek Nation mixed with Seminole Freedmen.
3. The 84 Slaves were the slaves of the Tiger Clan (Katevlke).
4. African Methodist Episcopal Church

BIBLICAL SCRIPTURE: JOHN 14:15

"if ye love me, keep my commandments."

PART XIV

CORNMEAL "HOECAKES" BREAD AND ACCOMPANIMENT

SECTION I

MENU

Potato Soup
Cornmeal Hoecakes

RECIPES

Potato Soup

Amounts	Ingredients
4 cups	potato, cubed
2 quarts	water
1 tablespoon	salt
4 cups	milk
½ cup	onions, chopped

Directions

1. Wash and cube potatoes. Put potatoes in water With salt. Bring to a boil.
2. Boil to tender and pour water off.
3. Add milk, onions and continue to cook until done.

Cornmeal Hoecakes

Amounts	Ingredients
4 cups	cornmeal
1 cup	flour
¼ cup	sugar
1 teaspoon	baking soda
1 teaspoon	salt
1 ½ cups	milk

Directions

1. In a bowl, mix together cornmeal With flour, sugar, baking soda and salt.
2. Stir in milk and pour in pan.
3. Cook until done.

SECTION II

SEMINOLE FREEDMEN

1890s(Approximate Time of Settling in Seminole County)
LITTLE COMMUNITY
(located 8 miles south of city of Seminole, in Seminole County.)
Named for Thomas Little, second Chief of Seminole Nation

1. Cities, Towns, and Communities: Little
2. Type of People: Former slaves of Seminoles
3. May have come up on the "Trail of Tears" with The Seminole Indians.

BIBLICAL SCRIPTURE: LUKE 6:46

"And why call ye me, Lord, Lord, and do not the things which I say?."

PART XV

CORNMEAL "HOECAKES" BREAD AND ACCOMPANIMENT

SECTION I

MENU

Smoked Beef Ribs
Cornmeal Hoecakes

RECIPES

Smoked Beef Ribs

Amounts	Ingredients
3 pounds	beef ribs
3 tablespoons	salt
2 cups	molasses
1 cup	vinegar
1 cup	water

Directions

1. Clean beef ribs and season with salt.
2. Roast on low coals.
3. To make sauce, stir together molasses, vinegar and water.
4. When ribs are almost done, cover with molasses mixture.
5. Slowly continue to cook ribs.

Cornmeal Hoecakes

Amounts	Ingredients
3 cups	cornmeal
1 ½ cups	flour
1 teaspoon	salt
1 teaspoon	baking soda
2 tablespoons	sugar
½ cup	water
½ cup	milk

Directions

1. In a pan, mix together cornmeal, flour, salt, baking soda and sugar.
2. Stir in water and milk.
3. Make into 8 patties.
4. Cook individual patties on a hoe in the fireplace.
5. Serve with beef ribs.

SECTION II

SEMINOLE FREEDMEN

1890s(Approximate Time in Settling in Seminole County.)
JACKSON COMMUNITY
West of Wewoka

1. Cities, Town and Communities: JACKSON COMMUNITY
2. Type of People: Freed Seminole Indian Slaves
3. May have traveled from Fort Gibson founded in 1854. Freed slaves settled in Fort Gibson before traveling to their land in Seminole County.
4. The ex-slaves were freed by the Seminole Indians in 1866.
5. The Jackson probably left Florida after the Third Seminole War 1855-58.
6. Church: Rockhill Baptist Church
7. Descendants: Ministers of the gospel.

BIBLICAL SCRIPTURE: MATHEW 7:21

"Not every one that saith unto me, Lord, Lord, shall enter the kingdom of heaven; but he that doeth the will of my Father which is in heaven."

PART XVI

CORNMEAL "HOECAKES" BREAD AND ACCOMPANIMENT

SECTION I

MENU

Pork Sausage/Gravy
Cornmeal Hoecake

RECIPES

Pork Sausage/Gravy

Amounts	Ingredients
2 pounds	pork loin strips
1	pod of red pepper, chopped
1 teaspoon	sage
1 teaspoon	black pepper
1 teaspoon	salt

Directions

1. Using a meat grinder, grind together pork strips, red pepper and sage.
2. Add black pepper and salt
3. Make into patties. Cook in pan. Fry on both sides.
4. Remove patties from pan. Add 1 tablespoon flour and cook.
5. Slowly add water and cook until mixture thickens. Season with salt and pepper.
6. Serve with hoecakes.

Cornmeal Hoecakes

Amounts	Ingredients
2 cups	white cornmeal
1 cup	flour
1 teaspoon	salt
1 teaspoon	baking soda
2 tablespoons	lard
1 ½ cups	milk

Directions

1. Stir together all ingredients.
2. Make into 8 patties. Cook each pattie on hoe in the fireplace.
3. Cook hoecake on both sides.
4. Serve with sausage and gravy.

SECTION II

SEMINOLE FREEDMEN

1893s(Approximate Time of Settling in Seminole County)
MEKASUKEY MISSION SCHOOL
(Located 3 miles southwest of city of Seminole in Seminole County.)
Site of Mekasukey Academy, a Seminole Indian school for boys.

1. Seminole Indian boys and slave boys attended the school.
2. A creek Indian word meaning where the Chiefs meet'
3. School attended by James Coody Johnson.

BIBLICAL SCRIPTURE: JOSHUA 24:15

"As for me and my house, we will serve the Lord."

PART XVII

CORNMEAL "HOECAKES" BREAD AND ACCOMPANIMENT

MENU

Baked Chicken
Cornmeal Hoecakes

RECIPES

Baked Chicken

Amounts	Ingredients
1	chicken, fryer, cut up
2 teaspoons	salt
1 teaspoon	black pepper
1 cup	flour
1 large	onion, thinly sliced
½ cup	water

Directions

1. Wash and cut up fryer.
2. Season with salt and pepper.
3. Roll in flour. Place in baking pan.
4. Cover with onions. Pour water in pan.
5. Cover. Bake in fireplace for 2 hours.
6. Add water if necessary. Serve with hoecakes when done.

Cornmeal Hoecakes

Amounts	Ingredients
2 ½ cups	yellow cornmeal
1 teaspoon	salt
1 teaspoon	baking soda
1 tablespoon	sugar
1 cup	buttermilk

Directions

1. In a pan, stir together cornmeal, salt, baking soda and sugar.
2. Stir in milk. Make into 8 patties.
3. Make an area in the coals in the fireplace convenient for cooking the patties.
4. Cook each pattie on a hoe in the fireplace.

SECTION II

SEMINOLE FREEDMEN

1898s (Approximate Time of Settling Seminole County)
EMAHAKE MISSION
School for girls
Located 5 miles south of Wewoka.

1. Cities, Towns, Communities: Private Indian girls school also for ex-slaves of Seminole Indians.
2. Types of People: Indian girls and ex-slave girls
3. Emahake a Seminole word means "girl school".

BIBLICAL SCRIPTURE: I JOHN I:9

"If we confess our sins. He is faithful and just to forgive us our sins, and to cleanse us from all unrighteousness."

PART XVIII

CORNMEAL "HOECAKES" BREAD AND ACCOMPANIMENT

MENU

Fried Pig's Ears Sandwiches
Cornmeal Hoecakes

RECIPES

Fried Pig's Ears Sandwiches

Amounts	Ingredients
8	pig's ears
2	onions, quartered
2 teaspoons	salt
3 quarts	water
3 tablespoons	lard

Directions

1. In a large pot, boil pig's ears, onions and salt in water until tender.
2. Remove cooked pig's ears from pan. Dry off.
3. Heat lard in a skillet. Fry each ear until crispy.
4. Make sandwich by placing each cooked ear between the bread.
5. Serve.

Cornmeal Hoecakes

Amounts	Ingredients
3 cups	white cornmeal
1 cup	flour
1 teaspoon	salt
1 teaspoon	baking soda
1 cup	buttermilk
¼ cup	onion, minced
¼ cup	green pepper, minced
2 tablespoons	lard

Directions

1. In a pan, stir together cornmeal, flour, salt, baking soda and buttermilk.
2. Stir in onion, green pepper and lard.
3. Make into 8 patties. Cook on top of a hoe.

SECTION II

SEMINOLE FREEDMEN

1870s(Approximate Time of Settling in Seminole County)
NOBLETOWN COMMUNITY

1. Cities, Towns, Communities: Nobletown Community
2. Type of People: Ex-Slaves from Carolinas, Texas and Georgia.
3. Emancipated by the Seminole Indians
4. Chief of Nobletown: Robert Noble
5. Names of People who may have come up with the Seminole Indians: Nobles, Glass, Beavers, Phillips, Crockettes, Gordons, MacDonalds and Bruners.
6. Church: St. Stephen's Baptist Church

BIBLICAL SCRIPTURES: ROMANS 10:9,10

"If thou shalt confess with thy mouth the Lord Jesus, and shalt believe in thine heart that God hath raised Him from the dead, thou shalt be saved. For with the heart man believeth unto righteousness; and with the mouth confession is made unto salvation."

PART XIX

CORNMEAL "HOECAKES" BREAD AND ACCOMPANIMENT

SECTION I

MENU

Boiled Pig's Feet
Cornmeal Hoecake

RECIPES

Boiled Pig's Feet

Amounts	Ingredients
6	pig's feet, cleaned, hair removed and washed
2 tablespoons	salt
2 cups	onions, quartered
2	potatoes, chopped
2 pods	hot pepper, chopped
1 gallon	water

Directions

1. In a large pot, place all ingredients in and bring to a boil. Cover.
2. Boil for 2 hours.
3. Serve each pig's foot with 2 tablespoons of vinegar and hoe cake.

ARON HUNT

Cornmeal Hoecakes

Amounts	Ingredients
4 cups	cornmeal, yellow
½ cup	flour
2 tablespoons	sugar
1 ½ teaspoons	baking soda
1 cup	sour milk

Directions

1. In a pan, stir together all ingredients.
2. Make into patties, and cook each patty on a hoe in the fireplace.
3. Serve with boiled pig's feet.

18

SECTION II

SEMINOLE FREEDMEN

1890s (Approximate Time of Settling Seminole County)
CAROLINA COMMUNITY
Southwest of Wewoka

1. Cities, Town, Communities: Carolina Community
2. Type of People: Seminole Freedmen from Carolinas.
3. Carolinas were known as warriors.

BIBLICAL SCRIPTURE: GENESIS 9:1

PART XX

CORNMEAL "HOECAKES" BREAD AND ACCOMPANIMENT

SECTION I

MENU

Smothered Chicken
Cornmeal Hoecakes

RECIPES

Smothered Chicken

Amounts	Ingredients
1	Chicken fryer, cut up
2 teaspoons	salt
1 teaspoon	black pepper
1/3 cup	flour
3 tablespoons	lard
1/3 cup	onion, minced
2 tablespoons	flour
3 cups	water

Directions

1. Wash and cut up chicken. Season with salt and black pepper.
2. Roll in flour. Dust flour off each piece of chicken.
3. Heat lard in skillet. Cook chicken until each piece is done.
4. Remove chicken and place on a platter. Place minced onion in skillet.
5. Cook for 2 to 3 minutes. Sprinkle 2 tablespoons flour in the skillet.
6. Gradually add water to skillet. Cook until mixture thickens. Season.
7. Add each chicken piece back to skillet and stir in the mixture.
8. Cover and slowly cook for 30 minutes. Serve with hoe cakes.

Cornmeal Hoecakes

Amounts	Ingredients
3 cups	yellow cornmeal
1/3 cup	flour
1 teaspoon	salt
1 teaspoon	baking soda
2 tablespoons	sugar
1 ½ cups	buttermilk

Directions

1. In a pan, stir together cornmeal, flour, salt, baking soda and sugar and buttermilk.
2. Make into 8 patties, cook on a hoe until done.
3. Serve with smothered chicken

SECTION II

SEMINOLE FREEDMEN

1870s(Approximate Time of Settling in Seminole County)
CUDJO COMMUNITY
Located northeast of city

1. Cities, Towns, Settlement: Cudjo Community
2. Types of People: Ex-Slaves of Seminole Indians
3. States from: Georgia, North and South Carolina
4. Possible Names of People who Settled the Area:
   Cudjo, Payne, Stephney, Lincoln, Carolina
5. Cudjo were known as fighters.
6. Cudjo Cemetery: Located southeast of Seminole Carolina,
   Cudjo, Edwards, Louie, Payne
7. Cudjoe was an interpreter and warrior.

BIBLICAL SCRIPTURE: GENESIS 22:18

"And in thy seed shall all the nations of the earth be blessed; because thou hast obeyed my voice."

PART XXI

CORNMEAL "HOECAKES" BREAD AND ACCOMPANIMENT

MENU

Smothered Pork Chops
Cornmeal Hoecakes

RECIPES

Smothered Pork Chops

Amounts	Ingredients
8	pork chops
2 teaspoons	salt
1 teaspoon	black pepper
2 cups	flour
½ cup	lard
3 tablespoons	onion, minced
1 cup	water

Directions

1. Wash, pat dry and season pork chops with salt and pepper.
2. Coat with flour. Set aside.
3. Heat lard and fry each chop on both sides.
4. Remove chops and place on a platter.
5. Cook minced onion for 2 to 3 minutes in the lard leftover from cooking pork chops.
6. Brown 2 tablespoons of flour in the skillet. Stir well. Gradually add water to skillet, cook slowly until mixture thickens. Add pork chops back to pan, cover and cook for 10 minutes.
7. Cool and serve with hoecakes.

SECTION II

SEMINOLE FREEDMAN

1870s(Approximate time of Settling)
DOSAR BARKUS COMMUNITY
(near Sasakwa)
Dosar Barkus Band -The Dawes Roll gave the band the name. Band composed of the slaves of John Jumper, Chief of the Seminole Nation-Fushutche Band(Bird Creek).

1. Cities, Towns, Communities:
2. Type of People: 17th Century English Carolinas slaves to Florida. William Noble was the head until 1898. The Band was emancipated by the Seminole Indians.
3. Probably left Florida after the Second Seminole War 1835-42.
4. Descendants: Barkus family
5. What relationship did Dosar Barkus have with William Noble?

BIBLICAL SCRIPTURE: EXODUS 9:1

"Then the Lord said unto Moses, Go in unto Pharaoh, and tell him, Thus saith the Lord God of the Hebrews, Let my people go, that they may serve me."

PART XXII

CORNMEAL "HOECAKES" BREAD
AND ACCOMPANIMENT

SECTION I

MENU

Fried Chicken
Cornmeal Hoecakes

Recipes

Fried Chicken

Amount	Ingredients
1	fryer, cut up
1 teaspoon	salt
1 teaspoon	black pepper
1 ½ cups	flour
2 cups	lard

Directions

1. Wash and pat dry chicken.
2. Season with salt and pepper.
3. Roll in flour.
4. Heat lard in skillet to hot.
5. Fry chicken until golden brown.
6. Serve with cornmeal hoecakes.

Cornmeal Hoecakes

Amounts	Ingredients
3 cups	coarsely ground cornmeal
1 teaspoon	salt
2 tablespoons	sugar
1 teaspoon	baking soda
½ cup	flour
1 cup	milk

Directions

1. Stir together cornmeal, salt, sugar, baking soda and flour.
2. Gradually add milk.
3. Make into patties and cook on hoe in the fireplace.
4. Cool and serve with fried chicken.

SECTION II

SEMINOLE FREEDMAN

1890s(Approximate Time of Settling in Seminole County)
PLEASANT GROVE COMMUNITY

1. Cities, Towns, Communities: Pleasant Grove community
2. Type of People: Freed Seminole Slaves
3. Church: Pleasant Grove Church

BIBLICAL SCRIPTURE: EXODUS 13:6

"Seven days thou shalt eat unleavened bread, and in the seventh day shall be a feast to the Lord."

PART XXIII

CORNBREAD "HOECAKES" BREAD AND ACCOMPANIMENT

MENU

Beef Bone Soup
Cornmeal Hoecake w Jalapeno Peppers

RECIPES

Beef Bone Soup

Amounts	Ingredients
2 pounds	Beef Bones
2 tablespoon	salt
2 quarts	water
1	tomatoes, chopped
2	potatoes, chopped

Directions

1. In a large pot, cook beef bones, salt and water for 2 hours.
2. Add more water if needed.
3. Add tomatoes and potatoes. Continue to cook

Cornmeal Hoecakes

Amounts	Ingredients
2 cups	cornmeal
½ cup	whole kernel corn
¼ cup	onion, minced
1 ½ teaspoons	salt
1	jalapeno, minced
1	egg, beaten
1 cup	milk

Directions

1. In a pan, stir together all ingredients.
2. Make into patties and cook each pattie on a hoe.
3. Serve.

SECTION II

SEMINOLE FREEDMEN

1890s(Approximate Time in Settling in Seminole County)
MIDDLE CREEK
Near Konawa
(Incorporated in 1904.)

1. Cities, Towns, Communities: Middle Creek
2. Types of People: Seminole Freedmen
3. Middle Creek Baptist Church

BIBLICAL SCRIPTURE: EXODUS 16:29

"See, for that the Lord hath given you the sabbath, therefore he giveth you on the sixth day the bread of two days, abide ye every man in his place, let no man go out of his place on the seventh day."

PART XXIV

CORNMEAL "HOECAKES" BREAD AND ACCOMPANIMENT

MENU

Smoked Calf
Cornmeal Hoecakes

RECIPES

Smoked Calf

Amounts	Ingredients
2- halves	calf
1 pound	lard
½ cup	salt
¼ cup	black pepper

Directions

1. Skin and clean calf. Split in half. Pat dry.
2. Rub with lard inside and out of both halves.
3. Season with salt and pepper inside and outside of meat.
4. Place on top of coals prepared for the cooking.
5. Cook slowly turning until desired doneness.

Cornmeal Hoecakes

Amounts	Ingredients
2 cups	cornmeal
2 cups	flour
1 teaspoon	salt
1 ½ teaspoons	baking soda
2 tablespoon	sugar
2 tablespoons	butter
1 cup	milk

Directions

1. In a pan, stir together cornmeal, flour, salt, baking soda, and sugar.
2. Stir in butter.
3. Gradually add milk.
4. Form into patties.
5. Cook slow on top of hot coals with a hoe. Cook on both sides.

SECTION II

SEMINOLE FREEDMEN

1890s(Approximate time in Settling in Seminole County)
Chapel Grove/Center(near Cromwell)
North in Seminole County
Freed through Emancipation Proclamation and the end of the Civil War.

1. Cities, Towns, and Communities: Chapel Grove Communities
2. Seminole Freedman: The land was gotten from the Seminole Indians and Dawes Roll number. Some of the people were emancipated by their white masters.
3. Possible emancipated slaves who lived in Centre: Fields, Coopers, Gilberts, Grays, Harden, Hightowers, Lacy, Wilsons
4. Where were the ex-slaves from? The ex-slaves came from Mississippi, Georgia, Texas, Alabama, North Carolina, Louisiana

PART XXV

CORNMEAL "HOECAKES" BREAD
AND ACCOMPANIMENT

SECTION I

MENU

Barbeque Goat
Cornmeal Hoecakes

RECIPES

Barbeque Goat

Amounts	Ingredients
1-20 pound	goat, cut into halves
2 tablespoons	salt
2 tablespoon	black pepper
2 cups	lard
1 cup	molasses
1 cup	vinegar
2 cups	water

Directions

1. Skin, clean and wash goat halves.
2. Season with salt and black pepper.
3. Rub lard on both halves of goat.
4. Slowly cook over open coal fire.
5. While goat meat is cooking, heat together molasses, vinegar and water.
6. Cook for 10 minutes and stir as mixture cooks.
7. Cook meat until almost done.
8. Mop meat with vinegar mixture and then continue to cook until desired doneness.

SECTION II

SEMINOLE FREEDMEN
1890s(Approximate Time of Settling in Seminole County)
PARKER'S CHAPEL COMMUNITY
South of Wewoka

1. Cities, Towns, Communities: Parker's Chapel Community
2. Type of People: Seminole Indian ex-slaves
3. Church: Parkers Chapel Baptist Church
4. Some of the People were Creek Freedmen and Mixed People.

BIBLICAL SCRIPTURES: EXODUS 20:1-18

1. "And God spake all these words, saying.
2. I am the Lord, thy God, which have brought thee out of the land of Egypt, out of the house of bondage.
3. Thou shalt have no other gods, before me.
4. Thou shalt not make unto thee any graven image, or any likeness of any thing that is in heaven above, or that is in the earth beneath, or that is the water under the earth.
5. Thou shalt not bow down thyself to them, nor serve them; for I the Lord thy God am a jealous God, visiting the iniquity of the fathers upon the children unto the third and fourth generation of them that hate me.
6. And showing mercy unto thousands of them that love me, and keep my commandments.
7. Thou shalt not take the name of the Lord thy God in vain: for the Lord will not hold him guiltless that taketh his name in vain.
8. Remember the sabbath day, to keep it holy.
9. Six days shalt thou labor, and do all thy work:
10. But the seventh day is the sabbath of the Lord thy God: in it thou shalt not do any work, thou, nor thy son, nor thy son, nor

thy daughter, thy manservant, nor thy maidservant, nor thy cattle, nor thy stranger, that is within thy gates:

11. For in six days the Lord made heaven and earth, the sea, and all that in them is, and rested the seventh day; wherefore the Lord blessed the sabbath day, and hallowed it.

12. Honor thy father and thy mother, that thy days be long upon the land which the Lord thy God giveth thee.

13. Thou shalt not kill.

14. Thou shalt not commit adultery.

15. Thou shalt not steal.

16. Thou shalt not bear false witness against thy neighbor.

17. Thou shalt not covet thy neighbor's wife, nor his manservant, nor his maidservant, nor his ass, nor any thing That is thy neighbor's.

18. And all the people saw the thunderings, and the lightnings, and the noise of the trumpet, and when the people saw it, they removed, and stood afar off.

PART XXVI

CORNMEAL "HOECAKES" BREAD
AND ACCOMPANIMENT

SECTION I

MENU

Boiled Dried Blackeyed Peas
Cornmeal Hoecakes

RECIPES

Boiled Dried Blackeyed Peas

Amounts	Ingredients
3 cups	blackeyed peas, dried
1	cured pig's tail
1	red pepper, dried and chopped
2 tablespoons	lard
2 ½ quarts	water
1 tablespoon	sugar
1 teaspoon	salt

Directions

1. Thrash and pick peas. Wash peas and place in a large pot.
2. Add remaining ingredients.
3. Cover. Place in fireplace and boil for 4 hours.
4. Stir occasionally until done.
5. Serve with hoe cake cornbread.

Cornmeal Hoecakes

Amounts	Ingredients
3 cups	cornmeal
½ cup	flour
2 teaspoons	salt
1 tablespoon	sugar
1 cup	milk

Directions

1. In a pan, stir together all ingredients.
2. Make into 8 patties, cook on both sides.
3. Serve with peas.

SECTION II

SEMINOLE FREEDMEN

1890s (Approximate Time of Settling County)
PETER SALEM COMMUNITY
East of Wewoka
Peter Salem was a soldier in the Revolutionary War.

1. Cities, Town, Communities: PETER SALEM COMMUNITY
2. Types of People: Seminole Freedmen and Emancipated blacks from Louisiana
3. Descendants: Buckners

BIBLICAL SCRIPTURE: LEVITICUS 19: 2

"Speak unto all the congregation of the children of Israel, and say unto them. Ye shall be holy: for I the Lord your God am holy."

PART XXVII

CORNMEAL "HOECAKES" BREAD AND ACCOMPANIMENT

SECTION I

MENU

Fried Rabbit Sausage Sandwich
Cornmeal Hoecake

RECIPES

Fried Rabbit Sausage Sandwich

Amounts	Ingredients
5pounds	rabbit meat, lean without bones
5	red peppers, dried
2 tablespoons	salt
1 tablespoon	sage
1 teaspoon	black pepper
¼ cup	flour

Directions

1. Skin, clean and wash rabbit meat. Take all meat from bones. Grind meat in meat grinder.
2. Place ground meat in a pan, Stir in all ingredients.
3. Grind meat and other ingredients again.
4. Make into 10 patties.
5. Fry in lard for 5 minutes on both sides.
6. Drain fat from cooked meat. Serve as filler in cornmeal hoecake sandwiches.

Cornmeal Hoecakes

Amounts	Ingredients
3 cups	cornmeal
½ cup	flour
1 tablespoon	sugar
1 teaspoon	salt
1 ½ teaspoons	baking soda
¾ cup	buttermilk or sour milk

Directions

1. In a pan, mix together cornmeal, flour, sugar, salt and baking soda.
2. Add milk and stir. Make into patties.
3. Place on hoe and cook until doneness is complete.
4. Split in half and place sausage in between. Serve.

SECTION II

SEMINOLE FREEDMAN
1890s(Approximate Time of Settling in Seminole County)
MADKINS SETTLEMENT
North of Wewoka

1. Cities, Towns, Communities: MADKINS COMMUNITY
2. Type of People: Seminole Freedman possibly by the Dawes Commission.
3. Location near the Wewoka Lake.

BIBLICAL SCRIPTURE: LEVITICUS 20:9

"For every one that curserth his father or his mother shall surely put to death: he hath cursed his father or his mother; his blood shall be upon him."

PART XXVIII

CORNMEAL "HOECAKES" BREAD AND ACCOMPANIMENT

SECTION I

MENU

Pork Sausage Patties
Cornmeal Hoecakes

RECIPES

Pork Sausages Patties

Amounts	Ingredients
2 pounds	lean and fat pork strips
1 tablespoon	salt
1 teaspoon	black pepper
1 tablespoon	sage
1 tablespoon	brown sugar
1 tablespoon	onion, minced

Directions

1. Using a meat grinder, ground meat once.
2. Add remaining ingredients, mix well and regrind with meat grinder.
3. Make into patties. Coat patties with flour.
4. Fry patties on both sides until done.
5. Serve as filler for hoecake.

Cornmeal Hoecakes

Amounts	Ingredients
2 cups	yellow cornmeal
¼ cup	flour
1 teaspoon	salt
1 teaspoon	baking soda
¼ cup	onion, minced
½ cup	buttermilk

Directions

1. Stir together all ingredients. Make into 8 individual patties.
2. Cook on a hoe in the fireplace until done.
3. Cut into half. Fill with sausage and serve.

SECTION II

SEMINOLE FREEDMEN

1890s(Approximate time of Settling in Seminole County)
NEW ADDITION SETTLEMENT

1. Town, Cities, Community: NEW ADDITION SETTLEMENT
2. Types of People: Seminole Freedmen
3. Descendants: Alexanders,
4. Possible Dawes Rolls
5. Possibly born before statehood: Native Oklahomans

BIBLICAL SCRIPTURE: LEVITICUS 20:22,23

"22. Ye shall therefore keep all my statutes, and all my judgments, and do them: that the land, whither I bring you to dwell therein, spew you not out.

23. And ye shall not walk in the manners of the nation, which I cast out before you: for they committed all these things: and therefore I abhorred them.

24. But I have said unto you. Ye shall inherit their land, and I will give it unto you to possess it, a land that floweth with milk and honey: I am the Lord your God, which have separated you from other people."

PART XXIX

CORNMEAL "HOECAKES" BREAD AND ACCOMPANIMENT

MENU

Peach Jam
Cornmeal Hoe cake

RECIPES

Peach Jam

Amounts	Ingredients
1 quart	peaches, canned
2 cups	sugar

Directions

1. Boil peaches in pan for 1 hour and then add sugar and cook on low for 1 hour.
2. Stir until mixture makes a stiff jam. Serve as filler in hoecake.

Cornmeal Hoecakes

Amounts	Ingredients
2 cups	cornmeal
1 ½ cups	flour
1 teaspoon	baking powder
1 teaspoon	salt
1 cup	milk
½ cup	butter

Directions

1. In a pan, mix together all ingredients.
2. Make into 8 patties. Place on top of Hoe and cook in fireplace until done.
3. Split each hoecake and place peach jam between patties.

SECTION II

SEMINOLE FREEDMEN

1890s(Approximate Time of Settling in Seminole County)
McELWEE SETTLEMENT
North of Wewoka

1. Cities, Towns and Communities: McELWEE SETTLEMENT
2. Type of People: Freedmen
3. Land possibly granted through Dawes Commission
4. Possibly came through Fort Gibson
5. Descendants: McElWees

BIBLICAL SCRIPTURE: JOSHUA 24:28

"So Joshua let the people depart, every man unto his inheritance."

PART XXX

CORNMEAL "HOECAKE" BREAD AND ACCOMPANIMENT

MENU

Oxtail Soup
Cornmeal Hoecakes

RECIPES

Oxtail Soup

Amounts	Ingredients
1 pound	oxtails cut-up(cow's tails skinned)
1 tablespoon	salt
½ teaspoon	red pepper
1 teaspoon	black pepper
¼ cup	flour
2 tablespoons	lard
1 quarts	water
4	red potatoes, chopped
1	onion, quartered

Directions

1. Skin, chop and wash cow's tail. Season with salt and peppers
2. Roll in flour. Set aside. Heat lard in skillet.
3. Brown meat in lard. Place meat, onions and potatoes with water in a pan.
4. Bring to a boil. Cover and cook on low heat for 2 hours. Test for doneness.

Cornmeal Hoecakes

Amounts	Ingredients
2 ½ cups	yellow cornmeal, roughly ground
½ cup	flour
1 teaspoon	baking soda
1 teaspoon	salt
2 tablespoons	lard
1 cup	hot water

Directions

1. In a pan, stir together all ingredients.
2. Make into 10 patties.
3. Cook each pattie on top of a hoe until done.

SECTION II

SEMINOLE FREEDMEN

1890s(Approximate Time of Settling in Seminole County.)
EDWARDS COMMUNITY
Located north of Wewoka

1. Cities, Towns, Communities: EDWARDS Community
2. Types of People: Seminole Freedmen
3. Land may have been granted by Dawes Commission
4. Descendants: Edwards

BIBLICAL SCRIPTURES: I SAMUEL 2:7

"The Lord maketh poor, and maketh rich: he bringeth low, and lifeth up."

PART XXXI

CORNMEAL "HOECAKES" BREAD AND ACCOMPANIEMENT

MENU

Fried Hamburger
Cornmeal Hoecake

RECIPES

Fried Hamburger

Amounts	Ingredients
3 pounds	hamburger
2 teaspoons	salt
¼ cup	flour
¼ cup	onion, minced
2 tablespoons	lard

Directions

1. In a pan stir together all ingredients, except lard.
2. Make into 8 patties.
3. Heat lard in a skillet.
4. Cook patties in the lard 5 minutes on both sides.

Cornmeal Hoecakes

Amounts	Ingredients
2 ½ cups	cornmeal, yellow
2 tablespoons	flour
1 teaspoon	baking powder
1 teaspoon	salt
1 tablespoon	sugar
2 tablespoons	lard
1 cup	milk
1	egg, beaten

Directions

1. In a pan, stir together all ingredients.
2. Make into 2" inch balls.
3. Place one ball at a time and cook on a hoe until golden brown.

SECTION II

SEMINOLE FREEDMEN

1890s(Approximate Time of Settling in Seminole County.)
SCIPIO COMMUNITY
North of Wewoka

1. Cities, Towns, Community: Scipio
2. Type of People: Seminole Indians freed slaves
3. Scipio Church north of Wewoka
4. Descendants: Sangos
5. Land acquisitions: Maybe Dawes Commission

BIBLICAL SCRIPTURE: 2 SAMUEL 22:31

"As for God, his way is perfect: the word of the Lord is tried: he is a buckler to all them that trust in him."

PART XXXII

CORNMEAL "HOECAKES" BREAD AND ACCOMPANIEMENTS

SECTION I

MENU

Tomato Gravy
Cornmeal Hoecakes

RECIPES

Tomato Gravy

Amounts	Ingredients
2	tomatoes
3 cups	water
3 tablespoons	lard
¼ cup	onion, minced
2 tablespoons	flour
1 teaspoon	salt
1 teaspoon	black pepper

Directions

1. In a pan, boil tomatoes and remove skins. Discard skins and water.
2. Chop tomatoes. Set aside.
3. In a skillet, heat lard and cook onions until tender.
4. Add tomatoes and 2 cups of water. Bring to a boil.
5. Make a paste with flour and water from cooking tomatoes.
6. Gradually add back to pan. Continue boiling until mixture thickens.
7. Add salt and pepper. Continue to until desired doneness.
8. Serve.

Cornmeal Hoecakes

Amounts	Ingredients
3 cups	cornmeal
½ cup	flour
1 teaspoon	salt
1 teaspoon	baking soda
2 tablespoons	sugar
3 tablespoons	lard
1 teaspoon	garlic, minced
1 cup	goat milk

Directions

1. In a pan stir together cornmeal, flour, salt, baking soda and sugar.
2. Stir in lard and minced garlic.
3. Stir in goat milk.
4. Make 8 cornmeal patties.
5. Cook on hoe.
6. Serve by placing about 2 tablespoons of gravy on top of each patty.

SECTION II

SEMINOLE FREEDMEN

1890s (Approximate Time in Settling in Seminole County)
SPENCER PLANTATION
1 Mile West of Wewoka

1. Towns, Cities, and Communities: SPENCER PLANTATION
2. Type of People: Seminole Freedmen
3. Possibly Dawes Commission land allotment

BIBLICAL SCRIPTURE: I CHRONNICLES 4:10

"And Jabez called on the God of Israel: saying. "Oh, that thou wouldest bless me indeed, and enlarge my coast, and that thine hand might be with me, and that thou wouldest keep me from evil, that it may not grieve me! And God granted him that which be requested."

PART XXXIII

CORNMEAL "HOECAKES" BREAD
AND ACCOMPANIEMENT

MENU

Fried Beef Steaks
Cornmeal Hoecakes

RECIPES

Fried Beef Steaks

Amounts	Ingredients
8	beef sirloin steaks
2 teaspoons	salt
1 teaspoon	black pepper
½ cup	flour
1 cup	lard

Directions

1. Wash steaks and salt and black pepper.
2. Coat with flour.
3. Heat fat in a skillet and fry on both sides until crispy.
4. Serve as sandwich with hoecakes.

Cornmeal Hoecakes

Amounts	Ingredients
3 cups	cornmeal
1 cup	flour
1 teaspoon	baking soda
1 teaspoon	salt
1 cup	milk
1	egg, beaten
½ cup	tomato, minced
¼ cup	onion, minced

Direction

1. In a bowl, stir together. Make into patties.
2. Cook until done on a hoe.

SECTION II

SEMINOLE FREEDMEN

1890s (Approximate Time in Settling in Seminole County)
ANDERSON SETTLEMENT
North in Seminole County

1. Towns, Cities, and Communities: ANDERSON SETTLEMENT
2. Type of People: Seminole Freedmen
3. Possible Dawes Commission land allotment.

BIBLICAL SCRIPTURES: PSALM 5:12

"For thou, Lord, wilt bless the righteous with favor wilt thou compass him as with a shield."

PART XXXIV

SUGGESTED MENUS FOR SEMINOLE FREEDMEN CHURCH GATHERINGS BEFORE OKLAHOMA STATEHOOD

SAMPLE DINNER ON THE GROUND-The big black pot was used as the major method of cooking large servings of food. Before statehood, church was held outdoors under arbors. The people usually had fire pits or fire places for ovens. They used hoes and shovels for stirring and cooking. They made their own knives and forks. They made bowls and plates from tree limbs or trunks. All members from churches involved would bring assigned

Cooked foods. Each family had from 3 to 5 black pots.

MENU

BARBECUED WHOLE HOG
SMOKED WHOLE CALF
BARBECUED WHOLE GOAT
FRIED FISH IN THE BLACK POT
FRIED CHICKEN IN BLACK POT
BLACK POT OF CHITTERLINGS
CURED HAM
BLACK POT OF BLACKEYED PEAS
BAKED SWEET POTATOES in ASHES
BLACK POT OF TURNIP GREENS
JARS OF HOT PEPPER SAUCE
HOECAKE CORNMEAL BREAD
SLICES OF SWEET WATERMELONS
BLACK POT OF BLACKBERRY DUMPLINGS
BLACK POT OF PEACH COBBLER
BEVERAGES
SWEET TEA
SWEET COFFEE
JUGS OF POST OAK GRAPE WINE (ADULTS ONLY)
JUGS OF PEACH CHOCK (ADULTS ONLY)

SNACK

BOILED PEANUTS

RECIPES

Barbecued Smoked Whole Hog

(100 servings)

Amounts	Ingredients
200 pound	hog (cleaned, washed and rinsed with vinegar water)
2 cups	salt
10	potatoes, quartered
3	onions, quartered

Directions

1. Prepare a 3' X 4' barbeque pit for cleaned hog.
2. Hog maybe gotten from a farm or butcher. Thoroughly, clean all parts of the hog-inside and out.
3. All meat to rest. Wash meat with vinegar water (1 gallon vinegar mixed in 2 gallons of water).
4. Sprinkle meat with salt inside and out place potatoes and onions in center of hog.
5. Place hog on rack in coals and top with coals and let cook for 20 hours.
6. Soak in barbeque sauce at last hour of cooking.

Barbeque Sauce

Amounts	Ingredients
5 gallons	molasses
4 gallons	water
1 gallon	apple cider vinegar
2 gallons	tomato juice
1 cup	salt
1 cup	black pepper
½ cup	red pepper
1 pint	honey

Directions

1. Cook all ingredients in big black pot for 4 hours. Cook slowly and cool before serving.
2. Stir well as mixture cooks. Soak meat in sauce before serving.

BARBECUED/SMOKED WHOLE CALF

(Servings 75-100)

AMOUNTS	INGREDIENTS
1-100 POUND	cut calf in half
2 pounds	lard
2 cups	salt

Directions

1. Build rack to hold each calf half. Mount racks over low heat for slow cooking.
2. Prepare water to keep from cooking to fast.

3. Wash and clean calf. Discard insides and head. Rub with lard inside and out. Sprinkle with salt. Let stand 30 minutes and then cook over low heat.
4. Serve in slices.

BARBECUED WHOLE GOAT

(Servings 100)

AMOUNTS	INGREDIENTS
1-50 POUND	whole cleaned goat
2 cups	salt
1 cup	lard
1 cup	black pepper

Directions

1. Clean, wash and dry goat. Cut into half. Rub salt inside and out.
2. Lightly rub lard on meat and add black pepper.
3. Cook over heat for 10 hours. Apply cooked sauce before serving.

Cook Sauce.

Amounts	Ingredients
10	tomatoes, cut up
1	onion, cut up
¼ cup	salt
1 gallon	water
2 gallons	molasses

Directions

1. In a black pot, cook tomatoes, onion, salt and water until a paste is made.

2. Add molasses and stir well. Cook for 3 hours. Stirring well.
3. Cover meat with sauce.

FRIED FISH

(Servings 200 people)

AMOUNTS	INGREDIENTS
50 POUNDS	CARP FISH
50 POUNDS	CATFSIH
5 POUNDS	SALT
2 POUNDS	BLACK PEPPER
10 POUNDS	CORNMEAL
10 POUNDS	LARD

Directions

1. Clean and wash fish. Cut up fish and season with salt and pepper.
2. Roll in meal.
3. Place lard in big black pot and heat to hot.
4. Cook fish; few pieces at a time until golden brown.
5. Serve hot.

BLACK POT OF FRIED CHICKEN

(Servings 50 people)

AMOUNTS	INGREDIENTS
10	chicken fryers, cut up
2 cups	salt
1 cup	black pepper
2 gallons	buttermilk
5 pounds	flour
15 pounds	lard

Directions

1. Wash and cut up chickens. Season with salt and black pepper.
2. Dip in buttermilk and then flour. Shake off extra flour.
3. Heat lard until hot. Fry few pieces of chicken at a time.
4. Check for doneness. Serve hot.

BLACK POT OF CHITTERLINGS

(Servings 50 people)

AMOUNTS	INGREDIENTS
200 pounds	chitterlings, cleaned and cut
10 pounds	onions, quartered
2 pounds	potatoes, quartered
1 cup	salt

Directions

1. Clean and wash chitterlings. Place in large black pot.
2. Fill with water. Add remaining ingredients, stir.
3. Cover and bring to boil and cook until done. Drain and serve hot.

BAKED HAM IN BLACK POT

(Servings 50 people)

AMOUNTS	INGREDIENTS
2 LARGE	CURED HAM
1 quart	molasses
10	green apples, sliced

INGREDIENTS

1. Clean and cover hams with molasses. Place in a black pot that has a rack in it to keep ham from touching the bottom and sides. Place apple slices around hams.
2. Cover and let cook over coals for 10 hours on low.

BOILED DRIED BLACKEYED PEAS WITH RICE

(Serving 100 people)

AMOUNTS	INGREDIENTS
5 POUNDS	dried blackeyed peas
5 gallons	water
5 pods	red pepper, cut up
¼ cup	salt
¼ cup	sugar
2 cups	lard
3 cured	pig's tails
2 pounds	rice, cooked

Directions

1. Place all ingredients except rice in a big black pot. Stir cover with lid.

2. Build fire so mixture can begin boiling and then cook for 2 hours.
3. Let cook until done. Cook rice in another pot. Serve cooked peas over rice.

BAKED SWEET POTATOES IN ASHES

(Serving 50 people)

AMOUNTS	INGREDIENTS
50	sweet potatoes, cured
2 pounds	butter

Directions

1. Cook sweet potatoes in low coals until all are done.
2. Wash ashes from potatoes and serve with butter.

BOILED EARS OF CORN

(Serving 50 people)

AMOUNTS	INGREDIENTS
50 ears	yellow corn, cleaned
5 gallons	water
1 gallon	milk
2 cups	butter
1 cup	salt

Directions

1. Peel and clean corn. Wash corn ears.
2. Make fire, place black pot on top and fill with water.
3. Add corn and remaining ingredients.

BLACK POT OF TURNIP GREENS

(Serving 50 people)

AMOUNTS	INGREDIENTS
10	cured ham hocks
50 bunches	turnip greens and bottoms
2 cups	lard
½ cup	salt
5 pods	red pepper, cut up
2 tablespoons	sugar

Directions

1. Prepare coals and boil ham hocks until done.
2. Prepare greens and peel bottoms and cut up.
3. Stir all ingredients in boiling ham hock pot.
4. Cover and cook for 3 hours.
5. Check for seasoning.
6. Serve.

HOECAKE CORNMEAL BREAD

AMOUNTS	INGREDIENTS
(servings 100 patties)	
20 POUNDS	corn meal
10 pounds	flour
2 cups	baking powder
1 cup	sugar
1 cup	salt
3 cups	lard
1 gallon	milk

Directions

1. In a big pot stir together corn meal, flour, baking poJARwder, sugar and salt.
2. Add lard and milk.
3. Make out 100 patties
4. Fry individual patties in hot lard in a big black pot.
5. Serve hot.

JARS OF HOT PEPPER SAUCE

AMOUNTS	INGREDIENTS
5 POUNDS	hot green peppers
2 gallons	apple cider vinegar
1 cup	salt

Directions

1. Prepare 6-one pint wide mouth pint jars. Wash peppers.
2. Place peppers in jars.
3. Cook apple cider vinegar and salt together for 30 minutes. Stirring occasionally.
4. Pour over peppers in jar. Seal.

BLACK POT OF BLACKBERRY DUMPLINGS

(100 servings)

AMOUNTS	INGREDIENTS
1.	Make Blackberry Dumplings into two steps.
DUMPLINGS	
5 pounds	flour
2 tablespoons	baking powder
¼ pound	salt
1 pound	lard

Directions

1. In a large pot stir together all ingredients. Make into 1- inch pieces.
2. Drop when instructed.

BLACKBERRY COBBLER FILLING

AMOUNTS	INGREDIENTS
10 gallons	blackberries
5 gallons	water
10 pounds	sugar
¼ cup	salt
3 pounds	butter

Directions

1. Pick and wash berries. Place in the large black pot, stir in water, sugar and salt.
2. Cook over coals for 30 minutes. Stir well.
3. Add in butter. Heat to boiling and add dumplings few at a time. Stirring after each addition.

215

BLACK POT OF PEACH COBBLER

(75 people)

AMOUNTS	INGREDIENTS
25 POUNDS	peach slices
10 pounds	sugar
½ cup	cinnamon
10 pounds	butter
1 gallon	water

DIRECTIONS

1. In a large pan, stir together all ingredients. Place half of the crust on the bottom And sides of the black pot.
2. Pour mixture inside crust and then place remaining crust on top.
3. Place black pot inside of fire and place coals on top of top. Cook on low for 1 hour.

PIE CRUST RECIPE

AMOUNTS	INGREDIENTS
5 pounds	flour
2 tablespoons	salt
2 pounds	butter
1 pint	water

Directions

1. Stir flour and salt together. Stir in butter and then work in water.
2. Pat crust out to fit bottom and sides of large black pot. The make top crust.
3. Follow directions of cobbler.

SWEET TEA

(100 people)

AMOUNTS	INGREDIENTS
2 cups	loose tea
5 gallons	boiling water
1-5 pound bag	sugar

Directions

1. In a large pot, boil tea in water for 10 minutes.
2. Remove tea leaves. Add sugar.
3. Test for desired sweetness. Serve with ice.

ADULT BEVERAGES

POST OAK GRAPE WINE

(Servings 25)

AMOUNTS	INGREDIENTS
10 pounds	post oak grapes
5 pounds	sugar
5 pound	water

DIRECTIONS

1. Wash grapes. Divide into 4 parts. Place equal amounts of sugar and water on grapes. Cover and let stand for 5 days.
2. Drain with cheese cloth. Destroy impurities. Store in clean jars for 2 months before serving.

PEACH CHOCK BEVERAGE

(Servings 25)

AMOUNTS   INGREDIENTS
10 pounds   cut up peaches, pits removed
5 pounds   sugar

Directions

1. Divide peaches and sugar up. Place in covered containers.
2. Store into dry and cooled place. This is a fermenting process.
3. After week, drain and discard peaches and drain juice into jars.

BOILED PEANUTS

(servings 50)

AMOUNTS   INGREDIENTS
5 gallons   water
15 POUNDS   GOOBER PEANUTS, picked and washed
2 POUNDS   SALT

Directions

1. Make fire around pot and add water.
2. Add peanuts and salt.
3. Bring to boil and cook for 20 minutes.

HOG HEAD CHEESE IN A BLACK POT

(100 servings)

AMOUNTS	INGREDIENTS
4	Hog's heads
6	pig's feet
6	pig's ears
5 gallons	water
10 pods	red pepper
2 cups	salt
5 gallon	apple cider vinegar
2 gallons	water
Strain	strained broth
4	onions, chopped
5	red pepper pods, chopped

Directions

1. Clean head, feet and ears. Wash well.
2. Make fire, place black pot over fire, put meat in pot and pour water over meat and red peppers and salt cover and boil until tender.
3. Cool meat. Chop meat and discard bones. Strain broth.
4. Stir all ingredients together and cook for 10 minutes. Cool and make into molds.

SECTION II

APPROXIMATE TIMELINE OF SEMINOLE FREEDMEN TO SEMINOLE COUNTY, OKLAHOMA

(African -Descent -Escaped Slaves, Freed by Spanish, Maroons, Mixed with Seminole Indians Freedmen, Estelusti-Indian for Black People from Florida to Indian Territory, Oklahoma Territory before Oklahoma Statehood)

Time Period	Activity
1500s	Citizens of Congo, Nigeria, Sudan
1600s	Sold in Slavery to America
1620s -1700s	Sold to White Masters of Rice Plantations in Virginia, Georgia, South Carolina, North Carolina
1689-1693	Escaped slaves and fugitives Received freedom
1700s	Abraham born in Florida in the late 1700s
1778	Creeks changed the Lower Creeks to Seminole Meaning emigrants -settled elsewere.
1790s	Fought in American Revolutionary War Seminole Freedmen were mixed with Seminole Indians, Spanish, Whites, and other groups in the Area: known as maroons
1790s	Escaped to Spanish Florida Fort Mose-the first free black community in the United States. They were very successful. Lived among Seminole Indians married and had Children. Angry white men tried to capture The Seminole Freedmen.
1800s	Freed by the Spanish-Slavery was outlawed Until Florida became a state.
1821	First Seminole Freedmen moved to Indian Territory
1817-18	First Seminole War

1829-37	Andrew Jackson, 7th President responsible for removal of Seminole Freedmen from Florida 1830 The Indian Removal Act 1832 Payne Landing Treaty took away land from Seminole Tribe and removed them to Indian Territory
1838	Trail of Tears-Five Civilized Tribes leaving the South for Oklahoma and Kansas 1848 John Horse discovered All Black town -Wewoka
1856	Treaty of 1856 -Seminoles settle in Seminole County. Wildcat(Coacoochee) an adviser to Chief Mikanopy. Wildcat did not want to live among the Creeks.
1861-1865	American Civil War
1870s	2 Black Seminole Bands and 12 Seminole Indian Bands Some of the Indian Bands had slaves. Most of the Seminole Indian Bands had Black Interpreters Because the Blacks could speak Gullah and Indian Languages. The Gullah was a broken English and Creole.
1866	Treaty of 1866 -Ex-Slaves served as light horsemen And white men. In the Treaty of 1866, the Indians Were told to give their former African slaves citizen Ship and rights. They were known as Indian Freedmen. A treaty is a legal document between the U.S. Government and other parties.
1870s	The United States Army issued a message to the Black Seminoles, Chief John Horse and his Warriors to come back from Mexico and Become Indian Scouts and help fight for the United States. John Horse led 200 people to Coahaula, Mexico for freedom.
1870-1914	Black Seminole Scouts from Seminole County fought in Oklahoma and Texas Indian Wars

1890s	Seminole Indians Boys (Mekasukey) and Girls (Emahake) Mission Schools. Seminole Freedmen attended
1890s	Dawes Commission Established
1907	Oklahoma became a state.

BLACK INVENTORS AND THEIR INVENTIONS

Inventors		Inventions
1.	PAPER	AFRICANS
2.	CHESS	AFRICANS
3.	ALPHABET	AFRICANS
4.	MEDICINE	AFRICANS
5.	Civilization	AFRICANS
6.	Aeroplane Propelling	James S. Adams
7.	Biscuit Cutter	A.P. Asbourne
8.	Folding Bed	L.C. Bailey
9.	Coin Changer	James A. Bauer
10.	Rotary Engine	Andrew J. Beard
11.	Car Coupler	Andrew J. Beard
12.	Letter Box	G.E. Becket
13.	Stainless Steel Pads	Alfred Benjamin
14.	Corn Planter	Henry Blair
15.	Cotton Planter	Henry Blair
16.	Ironing Board	Sarah Boone
17.	Pace Maker Controls	Otis Boykin
18.	Guided Missile	Otis Boykin
19.	Torpedo Discharger	H. Bradberry
20.	Street Sweeper	Charles Brooks
21.	Disposable Syringe	Phil Brooks
22.	Horse Bridle Bit	L.F. Brown

23.	Home Security System	Marie Brown
24.	Horseshoe	Oscar E. Brown
25.	Lawn Mower	John A. Burr
26.	Typewriter	Burridge & Marshman
27.	Train Alarm	R.A. Butler
28.	Image Converter	Geo. Carruthers
29.	FOR Radiation Detector	Geo. Carruthers
30.	Peanut Butter	Geo. W. Carver
31.	Lotions and Soaps	Geo. W. Carver
32.	Paints and Stains	Geo. W. Carver
33.	Pillow Utilizing Air/Water	Larry L. Christie
34.	Track Athlete Trainer	John Clarke
35.	Automatic Fishing Reel	George Cook
36.	Ice Cream Mold	A.L. Cradle
37.	Horse Riding Saddle	Wm. D. Davis
38.	Shoe	W.A. Deitz
39.	Player Piano	Joseph Dickinson
40.	Arm for Record Player	Joseph Dickinson
41.	Door Stop	O. Dorsey
42.	Door Knob	O. Dorsey
43.	Photo Print Wash Clatonia	J. Dorticus
44.	Photo Embossing Machine	J. Dorticus
45.	Postal Letter Box	P.B. Downing
46.	Blood Plasma	Dr. Charles Drew
47.	Toilet(Commode)	T.Elkins
48.	Furniture Caster	David P. Fisher
49.	Guitar	Robert Flemming, Jr.
50.	Ikenga Gyroplane	David Gittens
51.	IKenga/MKS Automobile	David Gittens
52.	Skooterboard	David Gittens
53.	Golf Tee	George F. Grant

54.	Motor	J. Gregory
55.	Lantern	Michael Harney
56.	Thermo Hair Curlers	Solomon Harper
57.	Space Shuttle Retrieval Arm	W.M. Harwell
58.	Ice Cream	Auguster Jackson
59.	Gas Burner	B.F, Jackson
60.	Kitchen Table	H.A. Jackson
61.	Programmable Remote Control	Joseph N. Jackson
62.	Video Commander	Joseph N. Jackson
63.	O.F. Cable w/ Artis Jenkins	Non-Metsheath
64.	Bicycle Frame	Issaac R. Johnson
65.	Sani Phone	Jerry Johnson
66.	Wrench	John A. Johnson
67.	Super Soaker	Lonnie Johnson
68.	Eye Protector	P. Johnson
69.	Egg Beater	W. Johnson
70.	Defroster	Frederick M. Jones
71.	Air Conditioning Unit	Frederick M. Jones
72.	Two-Cycle Gas Engine	Frederick M. Jones
73.	Industrial Combustion Engine	Frederick M. Jones
74.	Starter Generator	Frederick M. Jones
75.	Refrigeration Controls	Frederick M. Jones
76.	Bottle Caps	Jones & Long
77.	Clothes Dryer	John H. Jordan
78.	Electric Lamp	Latimer & Nichols
79.	Printing Press	W.A. Lavalette
80.	Laser Fuels	Lester Lee
81.	Pressure Cooker	Maurice W. Lee
82.	Envelope Seal	F.W. Leslie
83.	Window Cleaner	A.L. Lewis
84.	Pencil Sharpener	John L. Love

85.	Fire Extinguisher	Tom J. Marshal
86.	Lock	W.A. Martin
87.	Shoe Lasting Machine	Jan Matzeliger
88.	Lubricators	Elijah McCoy
89.	Rocket Catapult	Hugh Macdonald
90.	Elevator	Alexander Miles
91.	Gas Mask	Garrett Morgan
92.	Traffic Signal	Garrett Morgan
93.	Hair Brush	Lyda Newman
94.	Heating Furnace	Alice A. Parker
95.	Air Ship (Blimp)	J. F. Pickering
96.	Folding Chair	Purdy J. Sadgwar
97.	Hand Stamp	W.B. Purvis
98.	Fountain Pen	W.B. Purvis
99.	Dust Pan	L.P. Ray
100.	Insect Destroyer Gun	A.C. Richardson
101.	Baby Buggy	W.H. Richardson
102.	Sugar Refinement	N. Rillieux
103.	Pressing Comb	Walter Sammons
104.	Hair Dressing Device	Walter Sammons
105.	Clothes Drier	G.T. Sampson
106.	Cellular Phone	Henry Sampson
107.	Urinalysis Machine	Dewey Sanderson
108.	Hydraulic Shock Absorber	Ralph Sanderson
109.	Curtain Rod	S.R. Scottron
110.	Multi-Stage Rocket	Adolph Shamms
111.	Lawn Sprinkler	J. W. Smith
112.	Automatic Gear Shift	R.B.Spikes
113.	Refrigerator	J. Standard
114.	Mop	T.W. Steward
115.	Cattle Roping Apparatus	Darryl Thomas

116. Stairclimbing Wheelchair   Rufus J. Weaver

117. Polym. Water Paint   Morris B. Williams

118. Helicopter   Paul E. Williams

119. Fire Escape Ladder   J. B. Winters

120. Telephone Transmitter   Granville T. Woods

121. Electric Cut Off Switch   Granville T. Woods

122. Relay Instrument   Granville T. Woods

123. Telephone System   Granville T. Woods

124. Electro Mech Brake   Granville T. Woods

125. Galvanic Battery   Granville T. Woods

126. Electric Railing System   Granville T. Woods

127. Roller Coaster   Granville T. Woods

128. Electo Air Brake   Granville T. Woods

Source: The Black Inventions Museum-A Non-Profit Corporation, LA.CA 90076

PSALMS 91

He that dwelleth in the secret place of the secret place of the most High shall abide under the Shadow of the Almighty.

2. I will say of the Lord. He is my refugee and my fortress my God, in him will I trust

3. Surely he shall deliver thee from the share of the fowler, and from the noisome pestilence.

4. He shall cover thee with his feathers and under his wings shalt thou trust: his truth shall be thy shield and buckler.

5. Thou shalt not be afraid for the terror by night, nor for the arrow that flieth by day.

6. Nor for the pestilence that walketh in darkness: nor for the destruction that wasteth at noonday.

7. A thousand shall fall at thy side, and ten thousand at the right hand, but it shall not come nigh thee.

8. Only with thine eyes shalt thou behold and see the reward of the wicked.

9. Because thou hast made the Lord which is my refuge, even the most High, thy habitation.

10. There shall no evil befall thee, neither shall any plague come nigh thy dwelling.

11. For he shall give his angels charge over thee, to keep thee in all thy ways.

12. They shall bear thee up in their hands, lest thou dash thy foot against a stone.

13. Thou shall tread upon the lion and adder: the young lion and the dragon shalt thou trample under feet.

14. Because he hath set his love upon me, therefore, will I deliver him: I will set him on high, because he hath known my name.

15. He shall call upon me, and I will answer him: I will be with him in trouble: I will deliver him, and honour him.

16. With long life will I satisfy him, and shew him my salvation.

The Black Inventions Museum-A Non-Profit Corporation. LA, CA 90076

REFERENCES

1. Mulroy, Kevin: The Seminole Freedmen: A History. University of Oklahoma Press, 2009.
2. Oklahoma Archives, Oklahoma History Center, 800 Nazib Zuhdi Drive, Oklahoma City, Okla.
3. Holy Bible King James Version
4. Oral Histories Seminole Freedmen, Little River, Johnson Community, Nobletown, Lima, Seminole
   And Bruner Town. Oral Histories from Hunts and Hills.

Printed in the United States
By Bookmasters